THE
SOLAR
SYSTEM

TIM FURNISS

RAINTREE
STECK-VAUGHN
PUBLISHERS

A Harcourt Company

Austin   New York

spinning through space
THE
SOLAR SYSTEM

Other titles in the series:
The Earth ● The Moon ● The Sun

Cover photographs:
The nine planets of the solar system [main];
The probe *Galileo*'s descent into Jupiter's atmosphere [inset middle];
the comet Hale-Bopp photographed on June 23, 1995.

Published by Raintree Steck-Vaughn Publishers, an imprint of Steck-Vaughn Company

Printed in Italy. Bound in the United States.
1 2 3 4 5 6 7 8 9 0 05 04 03 02 01

Library of Congress Cataloging-in-Publication Data
Furniss, Tim.
The solar system / Tim Furniss.
  p.   cm.—(Spinning through space)
  Includes bibliographical references and index.
  Summary: Discusses the solar system and the planets in it, describing their location, characteristics, and moons.
  ISBN 0-7398-2740-5 (HC)
  0-7398-3092-9 (SC)
  1. Solar system—Juvenile literature.
  [1. Solar system. 2. Planets.]
  I. Brown, Carron. II. Bull, Peter. ill. III. Title.
  IV. Series.
  QB501.3.F87   2000
  523.2—dc21   00-021065

CONTENTS

A FAMILY OF PLANETS

Near the edge of a galaxy of a hundred billion stars in space, there is a small, ordinary star. This star seems quite unimportant compared with some much larger, brighter stars in our galaxy, the Milky Way. The star has a family of nine planets orbiting it. We call this star the sun. The sun and the nine planets that orbit it are called the solar system.

Five of the planets are quite small and rocky, and the other four are giant planets made up mainly of gases. More than six billion intelligent beings live on one of the rocky planets. This is the third planet from the sun, our planet Earth.

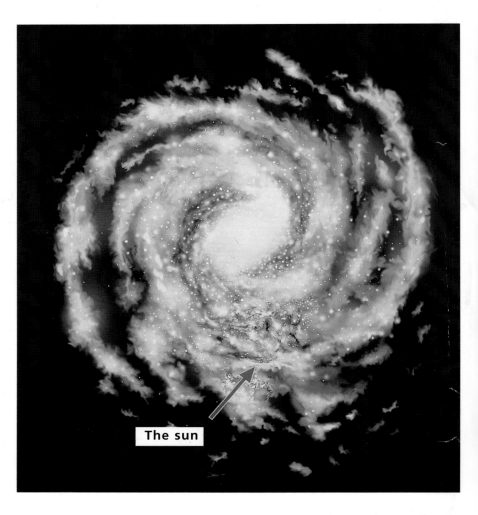

The sun

▲ Our galaxy, the Milky Way, with the sun's position shown by an arrow

It takes 5 hours and 20 minutes for light from the sun to reach Pluto. It takes 37,000 hours for sunlight to reach the nearest star, Proxima Centauri.

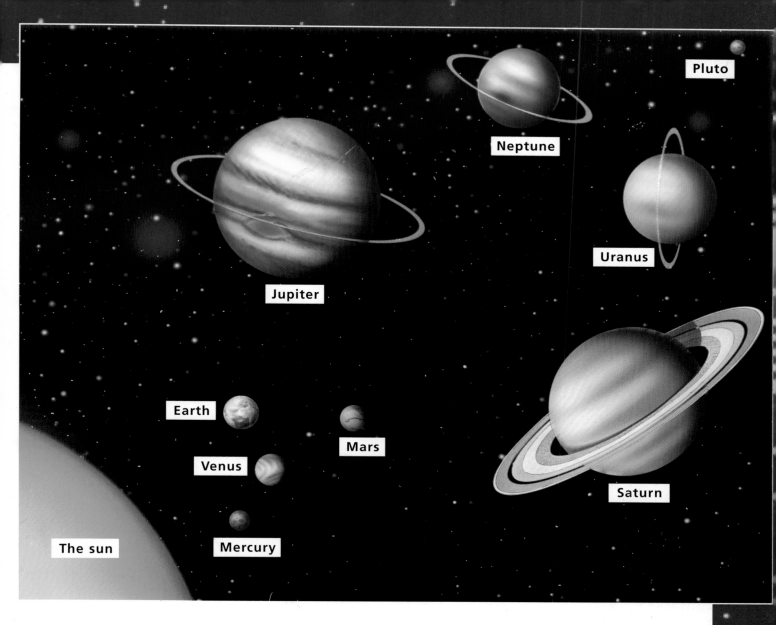

Pluto

Neptune

Uranus

Jupiter

Saturn

Earth

Mars

Venus

The sun

Mercury

▲ The planets of the solar system orbit the sun. "Solar" means having something to do with the sun.

Shooting stars are small meteoroids burning up in the Earth's atmosphere.

There are two planets, called Mercury and Venus, that are nearer to the sun than the Earth. The fourth planet from the sun is called Mars. Then come the four giant planets: Jupiter, Saturn, Uranus, and Neptune. The smallest and most distant planet is Pluto. In addition to the planets, there are other objects in the solar system: moons, rocky asteroids, comets, and meteoroids.

THE VAST UNIVERSE

The Earth and the solar system are a very small part of the vast universe. The sun is just one little star in the Milky Way galaxy. There are millions of other galaxies in the universe, too. We do not know how big the universe is.

To give you an idea of how large the universe is, distances in space are measured using the speed of light. Light travels at 184,925 miles (297,600 km) per second. It takes light from the sun 8 minutes 17 seconds to reach Earth. A light-year is the distance that light travels in one year— 5,878,764,100,000 miles (9,460,700,000,000 km). Light from Sirius, the brightest star in our night sky, takes about eight light-years to reach Earth. Light from the farthest object seen so far in the universe takes 13.2 billion light-years!

▲ Light from Andromeda, the nearest galaxy to us, takes 2.2 million years to be seen on Earth.

It would take more than 76 million years to drive a car to the star Proxima Centauri.

In 1995, the Hubble Space Telescope spotted what may be a solar system forming around another star.

▼ This picture from the Hubble Space Telescope shows a possible solar system in the making.

Astronomers believe that there could be other solar systems around other stars in the Milky Way. There may be solar systems around stars in other galaxies, too. It is not known yet whether any of these planets have any form of life. Life on Earth could be unique.

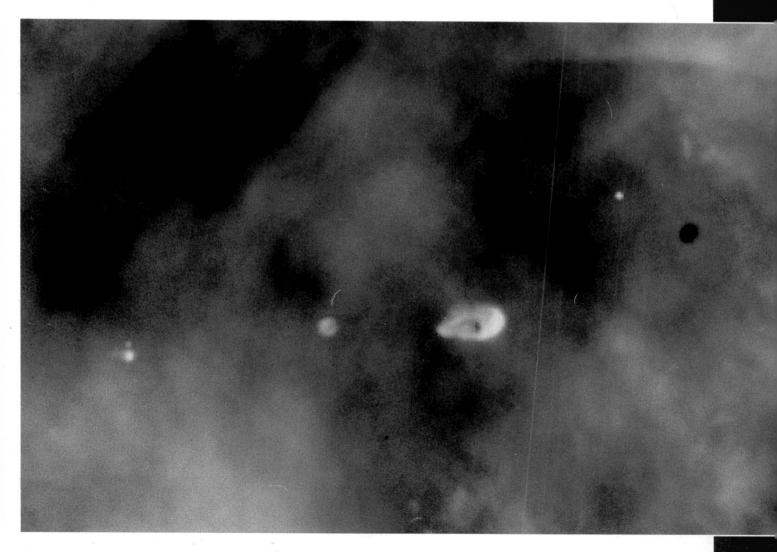

MERCURY

Mercury is the planet nearest to the sun. It is about half as far from the sun as Earth is. When Mercury comes its closest to the sun, the sun appears twice as large in the sky as it appears to us on Earth. There are extreme temperature differences on Mercury. The temperature in the intense sunlight is very hot at 788° F (420° C). The temperature at night is minus 292° F (minus 180° C)! There is no protective atmosphere on Mercury to provide air or to keep the planet at an even temperature. It would be impossible to live there.

If you put a can of baked beans on the surface of Mercury, the can would explode, the pieces would melt, and the beans would vaporize in the intense heat. If that can happen to a can of beans, imagine what would happen to you!

▼ Mercury is a small and rocky planet.

▲ Mercury's surface looks very similar to the surface of the moon.

Mercury takes just 88 Earth days to go once around the sun, a Mercury year. It rotates very slowly, once every 58 Earth days. A Mercury day lasts 176 Earth days!

Because Mercury rotates very slowly, the sun only rises and sets every two Mercury years. So the surface of Mercury has 176 days of sunlight and 176 days of darkness.

Nobody knew what Mercury looked like until a space probe called *Mariner 10* flew past in 1973 and took close-up pictures of Mercury's surface. These showed that it is covered with craters and mountains.

VENUS

The first close-up ▶ color photograph of Venus from *Mariner 10*, taken in 1974

Venus shows the "greenhouse" effect gone mad. This is due to the thick clouds of carbon dioxide in the planet's atmosphere. These trap the sun's heat on the surface and do not let the heat escape. Temperatures reach 887° F (475° C).

The atmospheric pressure, or the "weight" of the atmosphere, is ninety times that of Earth. It rains sulfuric acid. So, if you stood on the surface of Venus, you would be squashed, fried, and dissolved!

Even though the surface of Venus is so dangerous, some spacecraft have entered its atmosphere and survived long enough to send back pictures.

Venus reflects the sunlight brightly because of its thick clouds. This is why it is one of the brightest objects in the Earth's skies, along with the sun and the moon. Beneath the thick clouds, Venus has a surface of plains with flattened boulders and rocks. It has a highland region called Ishtar Terra that measures 1,802 miles (2,900 km) across. Venus also has mountains. Some mountains are higher than Mount Everest, the highest mountain on Earth.

The sun burns up 22 million tons of hydrogen each year. Scientists have calculated that the sun could go on shining for five billion years before it cools down.

▼ This image was created using a picture taken from above Venus by the *Magellan* spacecraft.

EARTH

Seen from deep space, the Earth is the brightest and one of the most beautiful planets. About three-quarters of its surface is covered by oceans of water that reflect sunlight. The Earth would look like a very bright, bluish star if seen from another planet.

The Earth is traveling through space at a speed of almost 18.6 miles (30 km) per second. In a year, the Earth travels a distance of 597 million mi. (960 million km).

Earth is unique among the planets. It is the only one on which we are sure life exists. The Earth has an atmosphere rich in oxygen and nitrogen. The atmosphere protects living things on Earth from deadly rays from the sun. The fast-moving clouds of water vapor in the atmosphere provide varied weather on the Earth's surface.

◄ This photo of a hurricane from above was taken by a space shuttle orbiting the Earth.

The Earth ▶
photographed by
Apollo 17 in 1972

Although
the Earth has a diameter of
7,926 miles (12,756 km), it has a very
thin crust, just 20 miles (32 km)
thick.

The Earth circles the sun in 365.25 days, an Earth
year. As it orbits the sun, the Earth is rotating
at a speed of 1,031 mph (1,660 kmph). In
24 hours, it makes one rotation, which is
called a day. The Earth has one moon,
which is 2,160 miles (3,476 km) in
diameter. It orbits the Earth at an average
distance of 238,861 miles (384,400 km).

MARS

Mars is a planet of canyons, volcanoes, dust storms, fog, frost, polar caps, and craters. Its atmosphere is 95 percent carbon dioxide and its maximum temperature is minus 20° F (minus 29° C). This is as cold as the coldest place on Earth. The atmosphere is too thin to keep the sun's heat on the planet's surface. Mars is not able to support life.

▼ *Mars Pathfinder* landed on Mars in 1997 to explore the surface and transmit pictures back to Earth.

▼ The largest of the volcanoes on Mars, called Olympus Mons, is 15.5 miles (25 km) high, five times as high as Mount Everest.

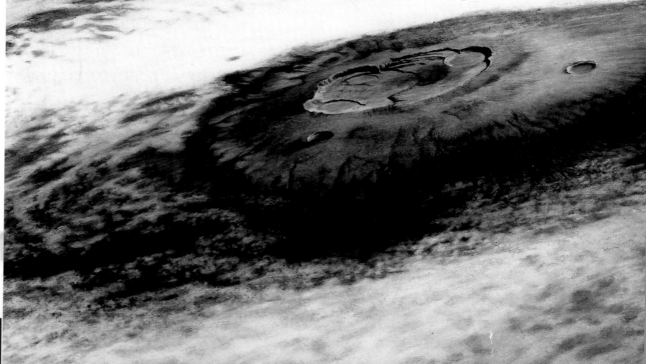

▲ Mars is called the Red Planet because of the rusty color of its surface.

The red color of the planet shows that its soil may contain iron oxide (the chemical name for rust). From the planet's surface, the Martian sky appears to be pink.

Mars has two moons that are huge rocks shaped like pock-marked potatoes. The moons are called Deimos and Phobos. Deimos is 9.3 miles (15 km) long and about 6.8 miles (11 km) wide, while Phobos is 16.8 miles (27 km) long and 11.8 miles (19 km) wide.

The polar caps on Mars are not like the polar ice caps on Earth. Martian ice is made mainly of frozen carbon dioxide gas. We call this "dry ice."

JUPITER

When the solar system and the sun were formed, Jupiter almost became another star. But it didn't get hot enough and has since cooled down. It is the largest planet in our solar system, measuring 88,734 mi. (142,800 km) in diameter. Jupiter is a huge ball of gases. Clouds of these gases spin quickly around the planet in under 10 hours. The surface of Jupiter is dominated by the Great Red Spot. It is a swirling hurricane of gases, with wind speeds of 21,748 mph (35,000 kmph).

▲ Jupiter and two of its moons photographed by *Voyager 1*

The Great Red Spot is 19,884 (32,000 km) long and 7,456 miles (12,000 km) wide. It could swallow up the Earth.

Jupiter has many moons orbiting it. There are four major moons. The moon Io is a frightening world of sulfur volcanoes. The surface of Europa is like a huge ice pack, under which there may be oceans of water. Ganymede has a surface that looks like a badly cracked eggshell. Callisto has a pock-marked surface that is like the outside of an avocado. Jupiter has at least 12 other moons, and there may be many more that are too small to see.

▼ A sulfur volcano on Io can be seen erupting on the horizon of the moon.

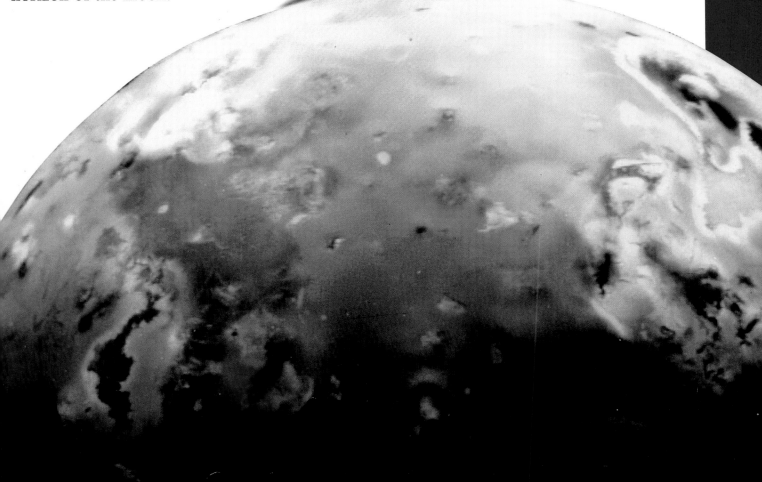

SATURN

The planet Saturn is probably the most beautiful planet in the solar system. It is like a smaller version of Jupiter, but it has a large ring system. Saturn's rings are made up of thousands of ringlets of small pieces of rock and ice. They are held together in an orbit by the planet's gravity.

Saturn is the second largest planet in the solar system. Its atmosphere is made up mainly of hydrogen gas. Under the clouds are lakes of liquid hydrogen.

Saturn's ring system is made up of "snowballs" of rock and ice, ranging in size from small flakes to 32.8 feet (10 m) in diameter.

▼ This magnificent close-up of Saturn's rings was taken by a *Voyager* spacecraft.

Saturn has at least 18 moons and may have more. Some are inside the ring system. The most famous moon is Titan. It has a diameter of 3,193 miles (5,140 km). Titan is the only moon in the solar system with an atmosphere, which has a thick mass of nitrogen and methane gas. Titan may have lakes of liquid gas on its surface. Another moon is called Mimas. This is only 242.3 miles (390 km) in diameter, but it has an enormous crater 80.7 miles (130 km) wide on its surface.

▲ This picture of Saturn and some of its moons was made using different pictures taken by *Voyager* spacecraft.

Saturn's rings are 170,882 miles (275,000 km) wide but only 328 feet (100 m) deep.

Neptune is a beautiful, ▶ blue planet. You can see the Great Dark Spot, which is four times the size of Earth. Hurricane winds blow around it.

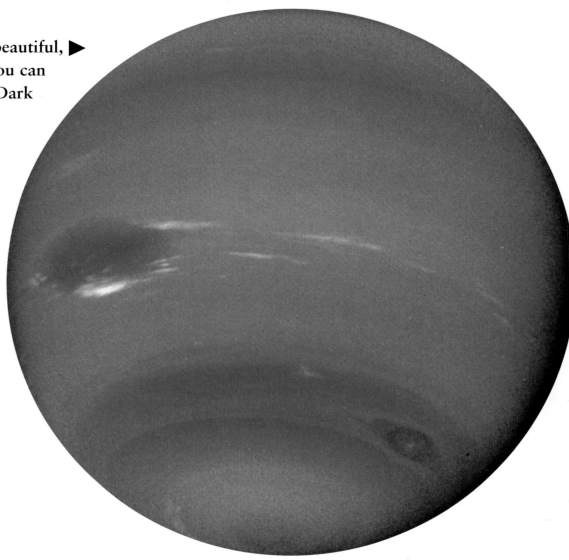

The farthest planets from the sun are Uranus, Neptune, and Pluto. Uranus is a planet of gases—mainly hydrogen and helium. It has poles that point almost sideways at an angle of 98° in relation to the plane of its orbit. This means that a point on the surface of Uranus has 42 years of daylight and 42 years of night.

Pluto's moon, Charon, is in an orbit that circles Pluto every 6.3 days. Charon appears stationary in the sky because Pluto rotates every 6.3 days.

Neptune is also a gaseous planet, with very strong winds. Scooter clouds in the upper atmosphere "scoot" around the planet at 1,491 mph (2,400 kph). This is faster than Neptune rotates. Neptune's two large moons are called Triton and Nereid.

Uranus was the first planet to be discovered using a telescope. It was discovered by William Herschel in 1781. All the other planets closer to the sun can be seen with the naked eye.

Rocky and icy Pluto, the smallest planet, has a moon, Charon, that is almost the same size. It is sometimes called a twin planet.

◄ Pluto is the farthest planet from the Sun. It may once have been a moon of Neptune that broke free.

▼ Uranus, seen in this artist's impression, has several rings around it and five moons.

ASTEROIDS, COMETS, AND METEORS

There are many objects of all shapes and sizes in orbit around the sun that seem to have been left over when the solar system was formed.

There are thousands of rocky asteroids. Most of these are in orbit between Mars and Jupiter. The largest asteroid is called Ceres. It has a diameter of about 470 miles (750 km).

The first recorded sighting of Halley's Comet was in 86 B.C. The comet appeared in A.D. 1066 at the time of The Norman Conquest of England. It is shown on the famous Bayeux Tapestry.

◀▼ The asteroid Gaspra (left) and the trail of a shooting star (below)

Other objects include comets, which are like "dirty" snowballs. When comets come close to the sun, they reflect the sun's light and we can see them. The sun's heat makes them evaporate, sending out a huge, steamy, bright gas trail. One of the most famous comets is Halley's Comet, which appears in the skies every 74 years. It was last seen in the night skies when it came close to the sun in 1986.

▲ A spectacular comet called Hale-Bopp shone brightly in the night skies in 1995–97.

It is possible to see about ten meteors or shooting stars an hour on a clear night.

Meteoroids come in many sizes. Most are the size of a really small pebble or grain of sand. Many enter the Earth's atmosphere every day. Usually, they are so small that they burn up while traveling at very high speed in the atmosphere. Meteoroids that do this are known as meteors, or "shooting stars." Sometimes, larger meteors have gone through the atmosphere and hit the Earth's surface. Some have been so big that they have formed huge craters.

SPACECRAFT EXPLORER

All the planets in the solar system except Pluto have been explored by unmanned spacecraft. Craft have landed on Venus and Mars. A probe has penetrated the atmosphere of Jupiter. Another craft is on its way to enter Saturn's orbit in 2004. *Mariner 10* is the only spacecraft to have explored Mercury. Many Russian and American spacecraft have been to Venus. Russian *Venera* craft have actually landed on its dangerous surface.

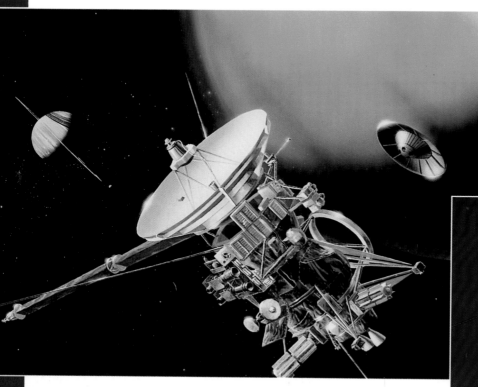

▲ This is how *Cassini* will look near Saturn as it detaches a craft to land on the moon Titan.

▼ *Mariner 2* made the first exploration of Venus.

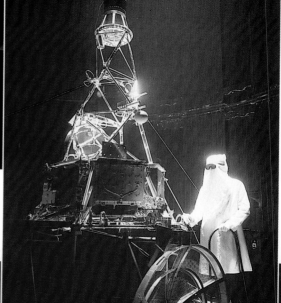

▲ *Galileo* sent a small probe into Jupiter's atmosphere in 1995.

Mars was first explored by a spacecraft in 1964, and the first landing there took place in 1976. More recently, the *Mars Pathfinder* landed in 1997.

The *Pioneer* and *Voyager* spacecraft have explored Jupiter and Saturn. One of the *Voyager* spacecraft has flown past Uranus and Neptune.

The first successful planetary space probe was *Mariner 2*, which flew past Venus in December 1962.

There are plans to launch new spacecraft to land on Mars. Some rocks from Mars may be returned to Earth about 2006 and analyzed for signs of possible life. Scientists plan to land humans on Mars one day. There are plans to launch a craft to explore Pluto. When it is launched, the craft will take more than 15 years to get there.

OBSERVING THE PLANETS

If you look up at the sky on a clear night, it is possible to see five planets, but not all at the same time. Many newspapers and magazines have special columns giving details of what planets can be seen and when.

▼ This photograph shows the moon, Venus, Saturn, and Jupiter in the night sky.

Mercury can sometimes be seen very low in the sky just after sunset. Venus is very bright in the evenings and mornings at various times of the year. Except for the sun and moon, it is the brightest object in the night sky. Its clouds reflect the sunlight very brightly.

Sometimes, planets appear so close to each other in the sky that they look like one bright star.

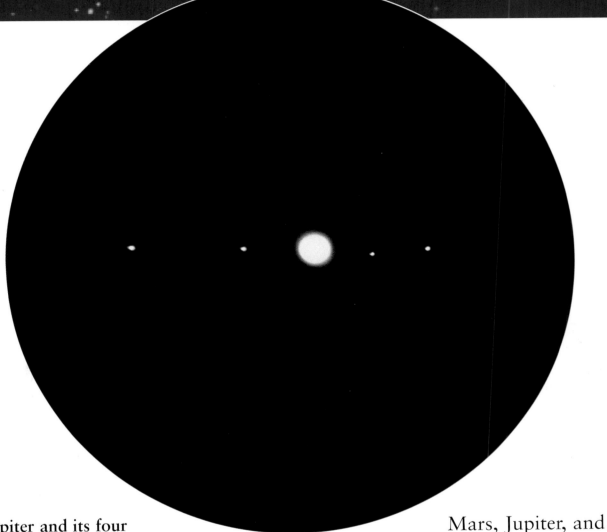

▲ Jupiter and its four main moons as seen through a small telescope

Venus can be so bright that it casts a shadow.

Mars, Jupiter, and Saturn seem to change their positions in the sky. This is because they orbit the sun at different speeds compared with the Earth, which is also moving around the sun. Mars looks like a red star in the sky. Jupiter can be very bright and rather yellow. Saturn also looks like a yellow star. With binoculars, it is possible to see the four big moons of Jupiter. With a small telescope, it is possible to see Jupiter as a very small globe. It is most exciting to see the rings of Saturn.

PLANET FACTS

	Diameter (miles/km)	Temperature (°F/°C)	Number of moons	Average distance from Sun (million mi/km)	Length of one rotation	Length of year/ orbit of Sun
Mercury	3,032/4,880	-292° to 788° /-180° to 420°	0	36/57.91	58 Earth days	88 Earth days
Venus	7,520/12,100	887°/475°	0	67/108.2	243 Earth days	224 Earth days
Earth	7,926/12,756	-128° to 120°/-89° to 49°	1	93/150	24 hours	365 days
Mars	4,217/6,787	maximum -20°/-29°	2	142/227.9	24 hours 37 minutes	687 Earth days
Jupiter	88,734/142,800	-193° TO 63°/-125° to 17°	at least 16	484/778.3	under 10 hours	11.86 Earth
Saturn	74,132/119,300	-285°/-176°	at least 18	887/1,427	under 11 hours	29.5 Earth y
Uranus	31,764/51,118	-357°/-216°	8	1,784/2,871	17 hours 23 minutes	84.01 Earth years
Neptune	30,776/49,528	-357°/-216°	15	2,794/4,497	16 hours 12 minutes	164.79 Earth years
Pluto	1,550/2,500	-382°/-230°	1	3,675/5,914	6 days 6 hours	248 Earth ye

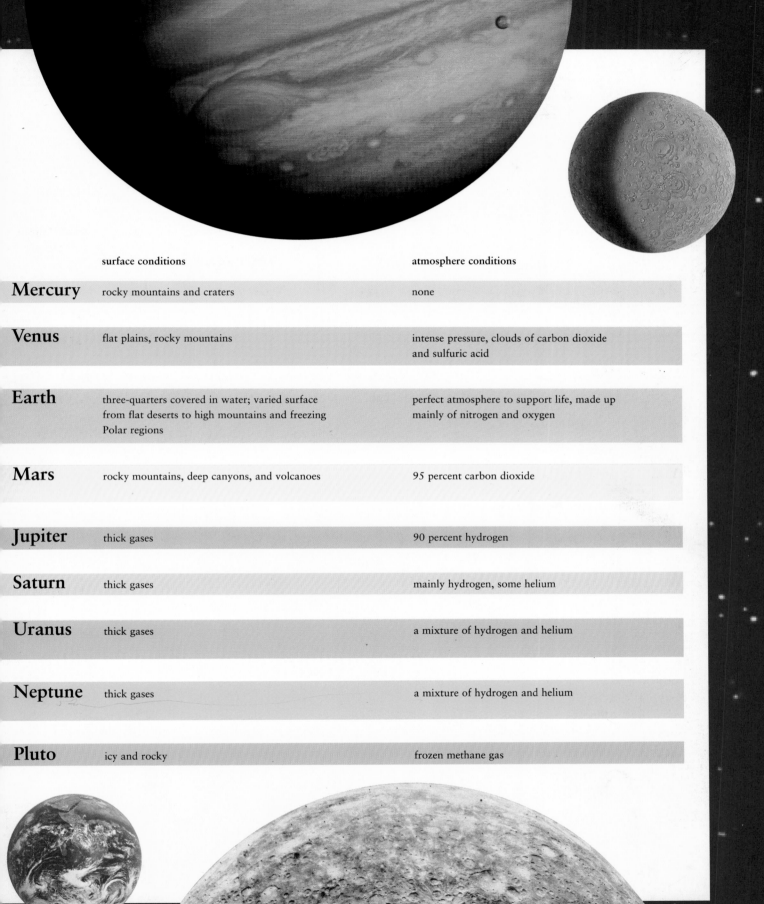

	surface conditions	atmosphere conditions
Mercury	rocky mountains and craters	none
Venus	flat plains, rocky mountains	intense pressure, clouds of carbon dioxide and sulfuric acid
Earth	three-quarters covered in water; varied surface from flat deserts to high mountains and freezing Polar regions	perfect atmosphere to support life, made up mainly of nitrogen and oxygen
Mars	rocky mountains, deep canyons, and volcanoes	95 percent carbon dioxide
Jupiter	thick gases	90 percent hydrogen
Saturn	thick gases	mainly hydrogen, some helium
Uranus	thick gases	a mixture of hydrogen and helium
Neptune	thick gases	a mixture of hydrogen and helium
Pluto	icy and rocky	frozen methane gas

GLOSSARY

Asteroids Small bodies of rock that orbit the sun.

Astronomer A person who studies the stars.

Atmosphere A layer of gas around a planet. Sometimes it can provide air; it protects a planet from the sun's rays during the day and can keep the heat on the surface at night.

Axis An imaginary line through the center of a planet around which it rotates.

Comets Traveling objects made of ice, dust, and other material. When close to the sun they leave a glowing tail of gas and dust behind them.

Craters Deep, wide holes on a surface.

Diameter The distance from one side of a circle or sphere through its center to the opposite side.

Galaxy A huge cluster of millions of stars.

Gravity A pulling force that brings two objects closer together. Smaller objects are drawn toward larger objects.

Greenhouse effect Atmospheric gases trapping the sun's heat and increasing the surface temperatures.

Meteor A streak of light produced by a meteoroid entering the Earth's atmosphere.

Meteoroid A solid object floating in space.

Moons Natural satellites that orbit planets.

Orbit To go around, or circle.

Planets Solid, spherical masses in space that orbit a star.

Probe An unmanned spacecraft that can gather and transmit information.

Solar system A group of planets that orbit a star.

Stars Large, luminous points in space that are spherical and made up of many different gases.

Sulfuric acid A substance containing the chemical sulfur that dissolves objects.

Universe Everything that is in space.

FURTHER INFORMATION

Websites:

photojournal.jpl.nasa.gov
NASA's planetary photo journal

www.nasa.gov/ This is NASA's homepage, which contains pictures and information about ongoing space exploration.

starchild.gsfc.nasa.gov/ Star Child: A Learning Center for Young Astronomers. This site is geared toward young people with an interest in astronomy.

Books to read:

Moore, Patrick. *The Starry Sky*. Copper Beech Books, 1999.

Platt, Richard. *Space Explorer Atlas*. Dorling Kindersley, 1999.

Sipiera, Paul P. *The Solar System*. Children's Press, 1997.

Vogt, Gregory L. *The Sun*. Millbrook, 1996.

Places to visit:

National Air and Space Museum
7th and Independence Ave., S.W.
Washington, D.C. 20560
(202) 357-2700
www.nasm.edu

NASA/Kennedy Space Center
Kennedy Space Center, FL 32899
(407) 452-2121
www.ksc.nasa.gov

INDEX

All numbers in **bold** refer to pictures as well as text.

Picture acknowledgments:
The publishers would like to thank the following for allowing us to reproduce their pictures in this book:
Genesis *cover* [inset middle], *contents page*, 7–13, 14 [top], 15, 17, 24 [both], 25, 28 [both], 29,
/NASA 18, 19, 22; Science Photo Library *cover* [main], *title page*, 26, /J. Baum & N. Henbest 4, /Lynette
Coote 21 [top], 29, /NASA 2, 14 [bottom], 16, 20, 21 [bottom], 29, /Pekka Parviainen
cover [inset bottom], 22, 23, /Rev. Ronald Roger 27; Topham *borders*, 6.
The illustration on page 5 is by Peter Bull.